BEST. RIDDLES. EVER.

JOKES for KIDS

CHANTELLE GRACE

BroadStreet KIDS

BroadStreet Kids
Savage, Minnesota, USA
BroadStreet Kids is an imprint of BroadStreet Publishing Group, LLC.
Broadstreetpublishing.com

Best. Riddles. Ever.

© 2020 by BroadStreet Publishing®

978-1-4245-6085-1
978-1-4245-6086-8 (ebook)

Content compiled by Chantelle Grace.

Design by Chris Garborg | garborgdesign.com
Editorial services by Michelle Winger | literallyprecise.com

Printed in the United States of America.

20   21   22   23   24   25   7   6   5   4   3   2   1

AUTHOR BIO

CHANTELLE GRACE is a witty wordsmith who loves music, art, and competitive games. She is also fascinated by God's intricate design of the human body. As a recent graduate from The University of Auckland with a degree in Nursing, she knows it's important to share the gift of laughter with those around her. While she grew up in the frozen tundra of Minnesota, she currently resides in the beautiful country of New Zealand where she works as a registered nurse.

NATURE

1) I go up
   when rain comes down.
   What am I?

2) I am the ocean.
   Where can you find me
   without water?

1) In the dark I am found
   without being fetched.
   In the light I am lost
   without being stolen.
   What am I?

2) I am a shirt.
   If you drop me
   in the red sea,
   what do I become?

3) The boy, girl, and their dog
   weren't under the umbrella.
   Why didn't they get wet?

4) I have lots of eyes
   but cannot see.
   What am I?

1) The stars. 2) Wet. 3) It wasn't raining. 4) Mississippi!

5

1) I am the letter of the alphabet
   that holds the most water.
   What letter am I?

2) I go around and around
   the woods,
   but I never go
   into the woods.
   What am I?

3) I come out at night
   without being called
   and disappear during the day.
   What am I?

4) I am the kind of tree
   you can hold in your hand.
   What am I?

4) A palm tree.

1) The letter C.   2) The bark on a tree.   3) The moon.

1) I am in the center of gravity.
   What am I?

2) A cloud is my mother,
   the wind is my father,
   my son is a puddle.
   A rainbow is my bed,
   and people often dislike me
   even though I am necessary.
   What am I?

3) When you take away more,
   I become bigger.
   What am I?

4) I have no feet, hands, or wings,
   but I fly to the sky.
   What am I?

1) I can be used to feed people,
   build houses, contain messages,
   and fertilize the ground.
   What am I?

2) If you feed me, I live,
   but if you water me, I die.
   What am I?

3) I am blue, red,
   and many other colors.
   I have no end,
   and no gold to find.
   I don't live in water or on land.
   If you could catch me,
   I would taste rather bland.
   What am I?

1) I grow in the winter
   but die in the spring.
   I am made of water
   but can hang upside down.
   What am I?

2) Before Mt Everest
   was discovered,
   I was the
   highest mountain
   in the world.
   What mountain am I?

3) You can see me in water,
   but I never get wet.
   What am I?

THE BODY

1) I have two legs
   but cannot walk.
   What am I?

2) I am a question
   you can never say yes to.
   What question am I?

1) When things go wrong,
   you can always count on me.
   What am I?

2) You can hear me,
   but you can't see or touch me
   even though you control me.
   What am I?

3) You can catch me,
   but you can't throw me.
   What am I?

4) I have teeth,
   but I cannot bite.
   What am I?

1) I am sitting in a dark house
   with no lights on,
   but I am reading.
   How is this possible?

2) I am as light as a feather,
   but even the world's strongest man
   can't hold me for more
   than a few minutes.
   What am I?

3) I have a thumb and four fingers
   but cannot pick anything up.
   What am I?

4) I am the best cure
   for dandruff.
   What am I?

1) I am reading Braille. 2) His breath. 3) A glove. 4) Baldness.

1) What do you call a man
who does not have
all his fingers on one hand?

2) I am the last thing you take off
before you get in bed.
What am I?

3) I have a bottom
at the top of me.
What am I?

4) I am moving left to right
and right to left
right now.
What am I?

1) Normal. (Most people have all their fingers on both hands.)
2) Your feet (off the floor). 3) Legs. 4) Your eyes.

1) I have legs but don't walk,
   a strong back but don't work,
   and two good arms
   but can't reach anything.
   What am I?

2) I have no legs,
   but I can run.
   What am I?

3) I weaken people
   for hours each day.
   I show you strange visions
   while you are away.
   I take you by night,
   by day bring you back.
   None suffer to have me
   but do from lack.
   What am I?

1) A chair. 2) A nose. 3) Sleep.

1) I have a tongue that can't speak,
   eyes that can't see,
   and a soul that can't be saved.
   What am I?

2) I run but never walk
   have a mouth but never talk.
   What am I?

3) A man walked all day long
   but only moved two feet.
   How is this possible?

AROUND THE HOUSE

1) I go up and down
   but never move.
   What am I?

2) I get wetter
   the more I dry.
   What am I?

1) If a red house
   is made of red bricks,
   and a yellow house
   is made of yellow bricks,
   what is a greenhouse made of?

2) I'm tall when I'm young
   and short when I'm old.
   What am I?

3) I am full of holes
   but hold a lot of water.
   What am I?

4) I have legs
   but don't walk.
   What am I?

1) Glass. 2) A candle. 3) A sponge. 4) A table.

1) In a one-story pink house,
   there was a pink person,
   a pink cat, a pink fish,
   a pink computer, a pink chair,
   and a pink table.
   What color were the stairs?

2) I run along your property
   and all around the backyard,
   but I never move.
   What am I?

3) Imagine you're in a room
   that is filling with water.
   There are no windows or doors.
   How do you get out?

1) There weren't any stairs. It was a one-story house. 2) A fence.
3) Stop imagining.

1) If Mr. Red lives in the red house,
   Mr. Green lives in the green house,
   and Mr. Black lives in the black house,
   who lives in the white house?

2) I have keys but no doors.
   I have space but no rooms.
   I allow you to enter
   but you can't leave.
   What am I?

3) I let you see
   right through a wall.
   What am I?

4) I have a neck, but no head.
   What am I?

1) The President. 2) A keyboard. 3) A window. 4) A bottle.

1) If you walked into a room
   with a lantern, a candle,
   and a fireplace,
   what would you light first?

2) I have one eye
   but can't see.
   What am I?

3) I need an answer,
   but I don't ask a question.
   What am I?

4) I have 88 keys
   but cannot open a single door.
   What am I?

1) A match. 2) A needle. 3) A phone. 4) A piano.

1) I can go up the chimney
   when I'm down,
   but I can't go down the chimney
   when I'm up.
   What am I?

2) I buried my flashlight.
   Why?

3) I am a door,
   but sometimes I'm not.
   When would that be?

4) I am an empty pocket,
   but I still have something in me.
   What is it?

4) A hole.

1) An umbrella. 2) Because the batteries died. 3) When I am ajar.

21

1) I leave home
   and turn left three times,
   only to return home
   facing two men wearing masks.
   Who are those men?

2) I make two people from one.
   What am I?

3) I have no breath,
   but I can die.
   What am I?

4) I am black, white
   and read all over.
   What am I?

1) The catcher and the umpire. 2) A mirror. 3) A battery.
4) A newspaper.

1) I have one head,
   one foot, and four legs.
   What am I?

2) I am a can that never
   needs a can opener.
   What am I?

3) I go up and down the stairs
   without moving.
   What am I?

4) I come in many different
   colors and shapes.
   I rise when I'm full
   but fall when I'm not.
   What am I?

1) A bed. 2) A pelican. 3) Carpet. 4) A balloon.

1) I hang or stand by a wall,
   run fast with hands
   but have no feet at all.
   What am I?

2) I always come into
   the house through a keyhole.
   What am I?

3) I come in different colors;
   sometimes I am hot,
   sometimes I am sweet.
   I'm sorry I can't answer you
   because even though I have a bell,
   it doesn't ring.
   What am I?

1) A clock. 2) The key. 3) Bell peppers.

1) I have feet on the inside
   but not on the outside.
   What am I?

2) Four rubber ducks
   were floating in the bathtub.
   Two floated away and two drowned.
   How many ducks are still alive?

1) Shoes. 2) Zero. Rubber ducks aren't alive and they can't drown.

25

IN THE KITCHEN

1) You have me for dinner
   but you never eat me.
   What am I?

2) I have to be broken
   before you can use me.
   What am I?

1) I am a room
   with no doors.
   What kind of room am I?

2) I have many layers.
   If you get too close to me,
   I'll make you cry.
   What am I?

3) I am a cup,
   but I don't hold water.
   What kind of cup am I?

4) I am a type of cheese
   that is made backwards.
   What cheese am I?

1) A mushroom. 2) An onion. 3) A cupcake. 4) Edam.

1) I am two things
   you can never eat for breakfast.
   What am I?

2) I am invisible.
   What do I drink at snack time?

3) I am put on a table and cut,
   but I am never eaten.
   What am I?

4) The sun bakes me.
   A hand breaks me.
   A foot treads on me.
   A mouth tastes me.
   What am I?

1) Lunch and dinner. 2) Evaporated milk. 3) A deck of cards.
4) Grapes.

1) Tuesday, Sam and Peter
   went out for pizza.
   After eating, they paid the bill.
   Sam and Peter did not pay the bill.
   Who did?

2) You throw away the outside
   and cook the inside.
   You eat the outside
   and throw away the inside.
   What did you eat?

3) You cannot see me
   nor can I be touched.
   You cannot feel me,
   but I can cook your lunch.
   What am I?

1) A car key opens a car;
   a house key opens a house.
   What opens a banana?

1) A monkey.

ON THE JOB

1) I start with P, end with E,
   and have a million letters.
   What am I?

2) I start to work
   only after I have been fired.
   What am I?

1) I go up
   but never come down.
   What am I?

2) This is the only place
   success comes before work.
   Where?

3) I fell off a 20-foot ladder
   but I wasn't hurt.
   Why?

4) I am the time you know
   you have to go to the dentist.
   What time am I?

1) Your age. 2) In the dictionary. 3) I fell off the bottom step.
4) 2:30 (tooth-hurty).

32

1) What is the difference
   between a jeweler and a jailer?

2) Today the sailors
   couldn't play cards.
   Why?

3) A lawyer, a plumber, and a hat maker
   were walking down the street.
   Who had the biggest hat?

4) If it takes six men one hour
   to dig six holes,
   how long does it take
   one man to dig half a hole?

1) A jeweler sells watches. A jailer watches cells. 2) The captain was standing on the deck. 3) The one with the biggest head. 4) There is no such thing as half a hole.

33

1) What did the outlaw get
   when he stole the calendar?

2) I am taken from a mine
   and shut up in a wooden case,
   from which I am never released,
   but I am used by almost everybody.
   What am I?

3) A building has four floors.
   The higher the floor,
   the more people live there.
   Which floor does the elevator
   go to most often?

1) I shave over 25 times a day
   but still have a beard.
   What am I?

2) I work when I play
   and I play when I work.
   What am I?

3) If four people can repair
   four bicycles in four hours,
   how many bicycles can
   eight people repair in eight hours?

TRANSPORTATION

1) I am the only time
   you go at red
   and stop at green.
   What time am I?

2) A truck driver is going opposite
   traffic on a one-way street.
   A police officer sees him
   but doesn't stop him.
   Why?

1) When you are eating watermelon. 2) The truck driver is walking.

1) I go up and down
   but never move.
   What am I?

2) I am an electric train
   heading south,
   which way is my steam blowing?

3) You walk across a bridge
   and see a boat full of people;
   yet there isn't a single person
   on board.
   How is this possible?

4) I go through towns and over hills,
   but I never move.
   What am I?

1) The temperature. 2) An electric train doesn't create steam.
3) All the people on the boat are married. 4) A road.

1) A cowboy rides into town on Friday,
   stays for three days,
   and leaves on Friday.
   How did he do it?

2) A man was driving his truck.
   His lights were not on.
   The moon was not out.
   Up ahead, a woman was
   crossing the street.
   How did he see her?

3) I am thrown out when you
   want to use me
   but taken in when you
   don't want to use me.
   What am I?

1) His horse's name was Friday. 2) It was daytime. 3) An anchor.

38

1) I am a ship with two mates
   and no captain.
   What ship am I?

2) I am so simple
   that I can only point,
   but I guide people
   all over the world.
   What am I?

3) I went out for a walk,
   and it started to rain.
   I didn't bring an umbrella or a hat.
   My clothes got soaked,
   but not a hair on my head was wet.
   How is this possible?

AROUND THE WORLD

1) What nationality are you
   on the way to the bathroom?

2) What nationality are you
   while you are in the bathroom?

1) What nationality are you
   when you leave the bathroom?

2) How is Europe
   like a frying pan?

3) I have streets but no pavement.
   I have cities but no buildings.
   I have forests but no trees.
   I have rivers but no water.
   What am I?

SPORTS

1) I am a race that is never run.
   What kind of race am I?

2) I threw a ball as hard as I could.
   It didn't bounce off anything,
   but it came right back to me.
   How did this happen?

1) A swimming race. 2) I threw the ball straight up in the air.

42

1) What did the baseball glove
   say to the ball?

2) You can you serve me
   but never eat me.
   What am I?

3) I am running in a race.
   I just passed the person
   in second place.
   What place am I in?

4) I am the fastest runner of all time.
   Who am I?

1) Catch you later.   2) A volleyball.   3) Second place.
4) Adam. (He was first in the human race.)

43

1) I am a boomerang
   that doesn't come back.
   What am I?

2) I love to move around,
   but usually not on the ground.
   I am strung out when way up high.
   I like to sail, but I need to stay dry.
   I need air, but not to breathe.
   A helpful hand is all I need.
   What am I?

ANIMALS

1) How far can a bear run into the woods?

2) How can a leopard change its spots?

1) Only halfway. Then it is running out of the woods.
2) By moving from one spot to another.

45

1) I am black, white,
   and blue.
   What am I?

2) I am orange and green
   and sound like a parrot?
   What am I?

3) I give milk
   and I have a horn,
   but I'm not a cow.
   What am I?

4) I am a key
   that can't open any door.
   What am I?

1) I am a dog catcher.
   How do I get paid?

2) How many animals
   did Moses take on the ark?

3) I am a dog.
   What do I have
   that no other animal has?

4) A dog was on a 10-foot rope
   but it got to a bone
   that was 12 feet away.
   How did the dog get the bone?

1) I am a person,
   but sometimes I'm like a snake.
   When would that be?

2) I travel very slowly
   when gliding along the ground.
   Maybe my shell weighs me down.
   What am I?

3) I have two heads,
   four eyes, six legs,
   and a tail.
   What am I?

4) I am what chimpanzees
   use to fix a leaky faucet.
   What am I?

1) I can jump and I can climb.
   With my many legs,
   I swing from tree to tree.
   I can build a house
   much bigger than me.
   What am I?

2) I am the type of music
   that rabbits like.
   What am I?

3) I have four legs
   but no tail.
   You often only hear me at night.
   What am I?

1) I am the month of the year
   when monkeys like to play
   basketball.
   What month am I?

2) There is a rooster on a roof.
   If it lays an egg,
   which way would the egg roll?

3) I peel like an onion
   but still remain whole.
   What am I?

4) I am always in armor,
   but I've never been at war.
   I have no sword, no bow, and no spear.
   What am I?

1) Ape-ril. 2) Roosters don't lay eggs. 3) A lizard. 4) A turtle.

1) A farmer has seventeen sheep.
   All but nine of them die.
   How many sheep
   does he have left?

2) I am a strange creature,
   hovering in the air,
   moving from here to there
   with a brilliant flare.
   Some say I sing,
   but others say I have no voice.
   What am I?

3) If three peacocks
   lay five eggs in eight days,
   how many peacocks
   will lay 45 eggs
   in 72 days?

1) Nine. 2) A hummingbird. 3) Peacocks don't lay eggs. Peahens do.

51

1) Emily loves cats and she
   keeps some as pets.
   All but two of them
   are completely black.
   All but two of them
   are completely white.
   All but two of them
   are completely ginger.
   How many cats does Emily have?

2) I am green
   but not a leaf.
   I copy others,
   but I'm not a monkey.
   What am I?

1) Three. 2) A parrot.

BACK TO SCHOOL

1) You see me once in June,
   twice in November,
   but not at all in May.
   What am I?

2) I am a word that
   becomes shorter
   when you add two letters.
   What word am I?

1) I am spelled wrong
   in every dictionary.
   What word am I?

2) A word I know,
   six letters it contains.
   Remove one letter
   and 12 remains.
   What word is it?

3) I contain 26 letters
   but only three syllables.
   What am I?

4) I am the month of the year
   that has 28 days.
   What month am I?

1) I am a band
   that never plays music.
   What am I?

2) There are four days of the week
   that start with the letter T.
   What are they?

3) I am the only place where
   Friday comes before Thursday.
   Where am I?

4) I begin and end
   with an E,
   but I only have one letter.
   What am I?

1) I can make one disappear.
   How?

2) Why is the letter T
   like an island?

3) I am an instrument
   you can hear but never see.
   What am I?

4) When I am white,
   I am dirty,
   and when I am black,
   I am clean.
   What am I?

3) Your voice. 4) A blackboard.
1) I add a G and it's gone. 2) Because it's in the middle of water.

56

1) Which is heavier:
   a ton of bricks
   or a ton of feathers?

2) How many letters are there
   in the English alphabet?

3) I am a number.
   Take away a letter
   and I become even.
   What number am I?

4) If two's company,
   and three's a crowd,
   what are four and five?

4) Nine.
2) 18. 3 in "the," 7 in "English," and 8 in "alphabet." 3) Seven.
1) Neither, they both weigh the same.
57

1) Draw a line.
   Without touching it,
   how do you make it
   a longer line?

2) Using only addition,
   I add eight eights
   and get the number 1,000.
   How?

3) What do the numbers
   one and eight have in common?

4) I have a large money box.
   Roughly how many coins
   can I place in my empty money box?

1) Draw a short line next to it, and now it's the longer line.
2) 888 + 88 + 8 + 8 + 8 = 1000. 3) They read the same right side up
and upside down. 4) Just one. After that, it will no longer be empty.

1) If you multiply me
   by any other number,
   the answer will always
   remain the same.
   What number am I?

2) I am a three-digit number.
   My second digit is
   four times bigger than
   the third digit.
   My first digit is three less than
   my second digit.
   What number am I?

3) How many seconds
   are there in a year?

1) Zero. 2) 141. 3) Twelve. January 2nd, February 2nd...

59

1) A school orchestra with six musicians can play Beethoven's Fifth symphony in seven minutes and 23 seconds. How long would it take to play if they doubled the number of musicians?

1) The same amount of time. The length of the piece of music doesn't change.

60

IN THE FAMILY

1) Emma's parents have
   three daughters:
   Snap, Crackle and...?

2) Mary has four daughters.
   Each of her daughters
   has a brother.
   How many children
   does Mary have?

1) Emma. 2) Five. Each daughter has the same brother.

1) Two fathers and two sons
   go on a fishing trip.
   They each catch a fish
   and bring it home.
   Why do they only bring
   three fish home?

2) Two children are born
   in the same hospital,
   in the same hour, day, and year,
   have the same mother and father,
   but are not twins.
   How is this possible?

3) A mother had five boys:
   Moses, Tucker, Webster,
   Thomas, and...?
   Was the fifth boy's name
   Frank, Evan, or Alex?

1) The men are a grandfather, father, and a son. 2) They are two of a set of triplets. 3) Frank. The first two letters of each boy's name begin with the first two letters of the days of the week.

62

1) A girl is 13 years old.
   Her father is 40 years old.
   How many years ago was
   the dad four times as old
   as the daughter?

2) A family of five people drove in a car
   for 300 miles at an average speed
   of 50 miles per hour.
   For the whole journey nobody noticed
   that the car had a flat tire.
   Why didn't anyone notice?

3) Tom owns an antique grandfather clock
   made in the year 1877.
   How long is it designed to go
   without winding?

1) A girl was 10
    on her last birthday,
   and will be 12
    on her next birthday.
   How is this possible?

WORD POWER

1) I am so fragile
   that saying my name
   breaks me.
   What am I?

2) I am easy to get into
   but hard to get out of.
   What am I?

1) I can be broken
   even if you never pick me up
   or touch me.
   What am I?

2) I am always in front of you,
   but I can't be seen.
   What am I?

3) I come once in a minute,
   twice in a moment,
   but never in a thousand years.
   What am I?

4) The more you take of me,
   the more you leave behind.
   What am I?

1) A promise. 2) Your future. 3) The letter M. 4) Footprints.

66

1) I am a word that looks the same
   backwards and upside down.
   What word am I?

2) If I have it, I don't share it.
   If I share it, I don't have it.
   What is it?

3) I am in seasons, seconds,
   centuries, and minutes,
   but not in decades, years, or days.
   What am I?

4) Forward I am heavy,
   but backward I am not.
   What am I?

1) I am always later
   and never present now.
   What am I?

2) The more of me there is,
   the less you see.
   What am I?

3) The rich men want me.
   The wise men know me.
   The kind men show me.
   What am I?

4) I have to be given
   before I can be kept.
   What am I?

1) I can bring a smile to your face,
   a tear to your eye,
   or even a thought to your mind,
   but I can't be seen.
   What am I?

2) I am greater than God,
   more evil than the devil,
   the poor have me,
   the rich need me,
   and if you eat me, you'll die.
   What am I?

3) I am yours to own,
   but others use me more.
   What am I?

1) Everyone needs me,
   asks for me,
   and gives me away,
   but almost nobody takes me.
   What am I?

2) I am greater than gold
   but cannot be bought.
   I can never be sold,
   but you can earn me if sought.
   Though I can be broken,
   I can still be fixed.
   I'm not started by birth,
   nor by death will I end.
   What am I?

3) Can you rearrange the letters of
   NEW DOOR to make one word?

1) Advice. 2) Friendship. 3) One word.

1) I am a word of five letters.
   People eat me.
   If you remove my first letter,
   I become a form of energy.
   Remove the first two,
   and I'm needed to live.
   Scramble the last three,
   and you can drink me.
   What am I?

IT'S A MYSTERY

1) The Wilsons' puppy was
   stolen on Sunday.
   The police know who took it
   by these clues.
   Can you figure it out?
   John was cooking.
   Alexis was getting the mail.
   Avery was planting in the garden.
   Kelly was doing laundry.

1) Alexis is guilty. There is no mail delivery on Sundays.

72

1) The Smith family is a
very wealthy family
that lives in a big, circular home.
One morning, Mr. Smith saw
a strawberry jam stain
on his new carpet.
Everyone had jam on their
toast that morning.
By reading the following excuses,
figure out who spilled the jam.
Mom: I was in the shower.
Billy: I was outside
playing basketball.
Maid: I was dusting the
floorboard corners.
Chef: I was making lunch.
Who is lying?

1) The maid. A circular house has no corners.

73

1) A boy was rushed to
   the hospital emergency room.
   The ER doctor saw the boy
   and said, "I cannot operate
   on this boy. He is my son."
   But the doctor was not
   the boy's father.
   How could that be?

2) Two men play five
   complete games of checkers.
   Each man wins the same
   number of games.
   There are no ties.
   How is this possible?

1) I am as small as an ant
   and as big as a whale;
    I can soar through the air
   like a bird with a tail.
    I can be seen by day
   and not by night;
    I can be seen
   with a big flash of light.
    I follow whoever
   controls me by the sun,
    but I fade away
   when darkness comes.
    What am I?

1) A shadow.

1) In marble walls
   as white as milk,
    lined with skin
   as soft as silk,
    in a fountain
   crystal clear,
    a golden treasure
   does appear.
    There are no doors
   to this stronghold,
    yet thieves break in
   and steal the gold.
    What is it?

1) A man lives on the 40th floor
   of an apartment building.
   When it is raining
   and he needs to go out,
   he takes the elevator down
   and the elevator back up.
   If it's not raining,
   he can take the elevator down,
   but he has to use the stairs
   to get back to his apartment
   unless someone else
   is in the elevator.
   Why?

1) The man is very short. If it's raining, he has an umbrella so he can
reach the button for the 40th floor. If someone is in the elevator,
he can ask them to push the button for him.

1) A man was going to town
   with a fox, a goose,
   and a sack of corn.
   He came to a river which he had
   to cross with a tiny boat.
   He could only take one thing
   across at a time.
   He couldn't leave the fox
   alone with the goose,
   or the goose alone with the corn.
   How did he get them all safely
   across the river and into town?

1) The man took the goose over first and came back alone. Then he took the fox across and brought the goose back. Then he took the corn. He came back by himself and took the goose.

1) Some chemicals were stolen
   from a chemist's lab one night.
   The only evidence was a piece
   of paper that had the names
   of chemicals written on it.
   The substances were nickel,
   carbon, oxygen, lanthanum,
   and sulfur. The chemist only
   had three people come by his
   lab on the day of the theft:
   fellow scientist Claire,
   his nephew Nicolas,
   and his friend Marc.
   The chemist knew who the thief
   was right away.
   How?

1) A Japanese ship was leaving the port.
The captain went to oil some parts
of the ship and took his ring off,
so it wouldn't get ruined.
He left it on his bedside table.
When he got back,
the ring was missing.
He thought of three crew members
who could be guilty. He went and
asked them what they were doing
when he was gone.
The cook said he was in the kitchen
getting dinner ready.
The engineer said he was in
the engine room.
The seaman said he was up
on the mast fixing the flag
because someone had put it on
upside down.
The captain knew right away
who the thief was.
How?

1) It was the seaman. The Japanese flag is white with a red circle in the middle. It can't be hung upside down.

80

1) On the morning before
   Christmas in NY,
   a mother went shopping.
   When she came home,
   the food in the house was gone.
   The youngest son said
   he was watching TV.
   The middle son said
   he was exercising.
   The oldest son said
   he was mowing the lawn.
   The dad said
   he was reading a newspaper.
   The mom knows who ate the food.
   Do you?

1) The oldest son. The lawn doesn't need to be mowed in the winter in NY.

1) A man is trapped in a room.
   The room has two possible exits:
   two doors.
   Through the first door there
   is a room constructed from
   magnifying glass.
   The blazing hot sun instantly fries
   anything or anyone that enters.
   Through the second door
   there is a fire-breathing dragon.
   How does the man escape?

1) A woman was sitting in her hotel room
   when there was a knock at the door.
   She opened the door to see a man
   whom she had never seen before.
   He said, "Oh I'm sorry.
   I thought this was my room."
   He then left.
   The woman went back
   into her room and called security.
   What made the woman
   so suspicious of the man?

1) He waits until nighttime and then goes through the first door.
2) You don't knock on your own hotel door, so the man was
probably lying.

82

SIGN LANGUAGE

1) What does this say?
   /R/e/a/d/i/n/g/

2) What does this say?
   STRAWBERRYcake

3) What does this say?
   sister

1) Reading between the lines. 2) Strawberry Shortcake.
3) Little sister.

83

1) What does this say?

L
A
Y
I
N
G
JOB

2) What does this say?
I RIGHT I

3) What does this say?
TOKEEPUCH

4) What does this say?
ESGG SGEG GEGS GSGE

1) Laying down on the job. 2) Right between the eyes.
3) Keep in touch. 4) Scrambled eggs.

1) What does this say?
   TOIMWN

2) What does this say?
   YYURYYUBICURYY4ME

3) What does this say?
   STOOD
   MISS

4) What does this say?
   POT OOOOOOOO

1) I'm in town. 2) Too wise you are, too wise you be. I see you are too wise for me. 3) Misunderstood. 4) Potatoes.

1) What does this say?
   GIVE
   GIVE
   GIVE
   GIVE

2) What does this say?
   OR OR NOTHING

3) What does this say?
   ZERO
   Ph.D.
   Ed.D

4) What does this say?
   1 END 3 END 5 END 7 END 9 END

1) What does this say?

ISSUES   ISSUES
ISSUES   ISSUES
ISSUES   ISSUES
ISSUES   ISSUES
ISSUES   ISSUES

2) What does this say?

ECNALG

3) What does this say?

T
O
W
N

LANGUAGE EQUATIONS

Figure out what these shortened phrases say.

1) 24 H in a D

2) 64 S on a C B

1) 12 M in a Y

2) 31 D in D

3) 1000 Y in a M

4) 23 P of C in the H B

1) 12 months in a year.   2) 31 days in December.   3) 1000 years in a millennium.   4) 23 pairs of chromosomes in the human body.

1) 1 L Y E F Y

2) 18 H on a G C

3) 4 S (S S A W)

4) 12 D of C

1) 1 leap year every four years.   2) 18 holes on a golf course.   3) 4 seasons (spring, summer, autumn, winter).   4) 12 days of Christmas.

1) 3 strikes you're out   2) 66 books of the Bible.   3) 60 seconds in a minute.   4) 90 degrees in a right angle.

4) 90 D in a R A

3) 60 S in a M

2) 66 B of the B

1) 3 S Y O

1) 10 Y in a D

2) 366 D in a L Y

3) 4 Q to the G

4) 60 M in an H

1) 10 years in a decade.   2) 366 days in a leap year.   3) 4 quarts to the gallon.   4) 60 minutes in an hour.

1) 9 I in a B G

2) 4 Q in a F G

3) S W and the S D

4) 360 D in a C

1) 9 innings in a baseball game.   2) 4 quarters in a football game.
3) Snow White and the seven dwarves.   4) 360 degrees in a circle.

1) 12 in a D

2) 7 W of the W

3) 88 K on a P

4) 12 I in a F

1) 12 in a dozen.   2) 7 wonders of the world.   3) 88 keys on a piano.   4) 12 inches in a foot.

1) 8 L on a S

2) 100 C in a M

3) 3 F in a Y

4) 10 Y in a D